BENJAMIN FRANKLIN
PRINTER AND PATRIOT

NEW
YORK

PHILADELPHIA

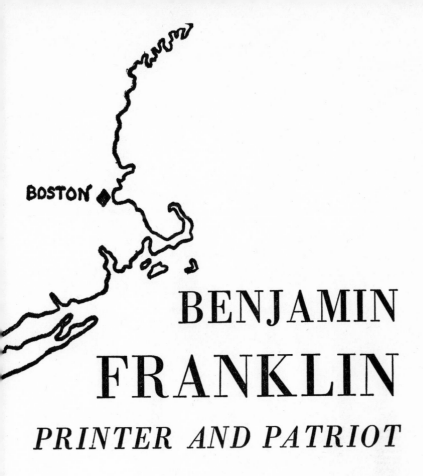

BENJAMIN
FRANKLIN
PRINTER AND PATRIOT

RUTH CROMER WEIR

Illustrated by Rus Anderson

Nashville   ABINGDON PRESS   *New York*

ISBN 0-687-02941-4

To my new daughter
Clarissa Lord Weir

THIS BOOK has been written with the help of many persons who have kept the memory of the real Benjamin Franklin alive. Grateful acknowledgment is made for the kindly advice of Morton Bodfish, trustee of the International Benjamin Franklin Society, and to his associate, Ralph J. Lueders. These men are especially interested in helping boys and girls to an intelligent understanding and practical application of Benjamin Franklin's philosophies, as valuable now as when he wrote them down, two and a half centuries ago.

RUTH CROMER WEIR

CONTENTS

CHAPTER ONE

• THE WORTH OF A WHISTLE •

Merry Christmas! Merry Christmas!

The joyous cry rang through the Boston streets. Sleigh bells jingled merrily. In the distance a horse whinnied, and there was the sound of happy laughter. Tunes of the old English carols still floated through the air, and Ben Franklin, seven years old, hummed softly.

A bright moon shone on the white ground and peaked housetops. Ben lagged behind his twelve brothers and sisters who still lived at home. He liked to hear the sound of the snow crunching under his feet.

Ben watched the others enter the door

where a blue ball, the sign of the candle-maker, hung above. Then his mother called. Ben stomped the snow from his boots and followed the others into the house.

"It has been a happy evening, hasn't it, Josiah?" Ben's mother was speaking to his father. "The carols never seemed more beautiful. And you played so well, Papa."

Ben watched his father put his violin case in the corner. Josiah Franklin often played hymns at home in the evening, but it was a rare occasion when he took his violin out of the house. Tonight Ben saw that his father's face looked pink and happy.

Suddenly one of the older Franklin children shouted, "Let's have parched corn! Stir up the fire! Get the kettles ready!" The big room buzzed with excitement as Ben's brothers and sisters rushed about. His favorite sister, Sally, told each one what to do.

The kettles were warming on the crane

in the big fireplace. "Keep shaking the kettles," Sally directed. "Listen!"

Pop. . . . . pop . . . . pop-pop . . pop-pop-pop-pop came the welcome sound of the dry corn breaking through its skin.

"Ben, get the butter bowl," cried Sally.

Ben dashed to the back porch and brought the huge wooden oval bowl his mother used for making butter. It was heavy for him to carry; he put it on the table with a thud.

Sally smiled and patted him on the head.

"Ready?" she asked. The others brought the kettles to the table and dumped the golden corn into the bowl. Then Sally poured sizzling melted butter over it all and stirred.

"*Mmmm*," the young folks murmured as they dipped hungrily into the big bowl.

A knock sounded at the door.

"It's the pastor," someone whispered.

"Come in. Come in, Reverend." Ben's father rose from his chair to welcome the guest. "You're just in time. Our food is plain. But the good company we have to visit us always makes up for that."

On the long table were rosy apples and chunks of maple sugar. But Ben almost forgot what he was eating, the conversation was so interesting.

Ben tried to keep awake. He tried to think of what he would buy with the coins he had been given for the holiday. Even that did not work. His eyelids felt heavier and heavier. Before long the warmth of the friendly room seemed to close around him. The voices sounded farther and farther away. Ben put his head on his arm and fell fast asleep.

The next morning Ben skipped gaily down the street. The slippery snow made skipping more fun than usual. The coins in his pocket jingled. Ben felt the pennies and halfpennies. He began to think of what he might buy with his money.

Suddenly he heard a loud, shrill noise. An older boy burst from a house down the street, blowing a whistle. Ben stopped.

The boy's cheeks puffed out and his face turned red. He blew the whistle as though he would never stop.

Ben was impressed. "Where did you get it?" he asked.

The boy paid no attention.

"Where did you get that whistle?" Ben screamed.

The boy seemed annoyed to stop blowing the whistle even for a moment. But he took it from his mouth just long enough to answer, "At the store."

"The store!" Ben spun around and began to run. Now he knew what he would buy with his coppers. A whistle.

Ben was excited and out of breath when he reached the store. He had been there a few times with Sally, but never alone. He reached up to lift the latch and open the door. As he went in, a little bell above the door tinkled softly. Ben walked past the big barrels on the floor. Before, he had peeped inside to see the sugar, salt, tea, and pickles in them. This time he was not interested.

At the counter Ben hesitated. Some bright new pocketknives caught his attention, but only for a moment. "I want a whistle," he said. "A real loud whistle."

"Do you have any money?" the store-keeper asked.

Proudly Ben dug in his pocket and pulled out his coins — all of them.

The storekeeper looked surprised to see a small boy with so much money. Quickly he reached behind the counter and brought out several bright-colored whistles. "There you are. Take your pick," he said.

Ben picked up the first one and blew. The whistle made a loud, shrill noise. Ben left the store blowing happily. "Now I can make as much noise as that boy," he said proudly. "I can make as much noise as *anybody*."

All the way home Ben blew his whistle. It made a screeching, ear-splitting noise. Ben loved it! Down the street and right into the Franklin house, Ben blew. And he kept right on blowing.

"Horrors!" Big brother James put his hands over his ears. And Sally asked, "Dear me, Ben, wherever did you get such a noise-maker?"

"I bought it," answered Ben. "I bought it with my holiday money."

"You spent all your money for that crazy whistle?" one of Ben's brothers asked. "You spent your four pennies and two halfpennies?"

Ben nodded.

"Why, you spent four times what it was worth!"

Suddenly everyone was staring at him. Ben felt alone in a room full of people.

Then someone began to laugh. Ben could bear it no longer. Tears filled his eyes. He loved that whistle. He had spent all his money for it. Was the whistle no good? He thought he had never been so miserable. Ben started to run to his mother. He knew she would comfort him.

"What's this all about?" Ben's father had come into the room. "If it's a joke, I'd like to laugh, too. But it seems to be at your brother's expense." Mr. Franklin looked sternly at Ben's brothers and sisters.

The laughter stopped as quickly as it had started. Everyone began explaining at once. "Ben spent all his money for that silly whistle." . . . "He paid too much for his whistle!"

The words rang over and over in Ben's ears. "He paid too much for his whistle!"

Ben's father found out the whole story.

He lifted Ben onto his lap. He took a big handkerchief from a pocket and began to wipe away Ben's tears. Ben's questioning gray eyes met his father's. His father was wise and kind and good. Whatever his father said, Ben knew he would believe.

Mr. Franklin never tried to keep the truth from his son. He nodded his head. "Yes, you paid too much for the whistle," he said at last.

Then Ben knew that it was true. He had paid too much for the whistle. He never wanted to blow that whistle again. He never wanted to see it again.

For a long time Ben thought about the whistle. Finally he made a promise to himself. "I will never again pay too much — for anything!"

CHAPTER TWO

• BOYHOOD ADVENTURES •

While Ben was growing up there was always plenty of work to be done in the Franklin home. "Fetch this." . . . "Take that." . . . "Run, bring some wood!" These were chores that were likely to fall to Ben as the youngest boy in a big family. But wide-awake Ben found plenty of other more exciting things to do, also. And there was always a group of boys eager to follow in whatever he wanted to do.

The seaport town of Boston and the marshes nearby held much to interest Ben and his friends. "Playing in the water is the most fun," Ben said. Paddling around in the salty marshes he learned to handle boats and to swim when he was very young. He became a good swimmer. "But I want to swim better and faster," he told his playmates. He watched the fish swimming in the bay. He watched and felt the oars as they sent the boat swiftly through the water.

One day Ben decided to make something like a fish's fins or the oars of a boat to help him swim faster. He carved some paddles from flat pieces of wood. Ben's friends laughed at his invention. But they watched eagerly when he slipped out of his clothes and tied the paddles to his hands and feet.

"Who will race me?" Ben asked. "I'll prove my invention is good."

"I will." . . . "I will." Several of Ben's friends were anxious to race. The other boys were to stay on shore to judge the race.

"All right," said Ben, "I'll race you out to that big rock and back. One, two, three, go!" Into the water Ben splashed, paddles and all.

For a few minutes Ben had a hard time getting his arms and legs to make the paddles move. Then he began to shoot ahead.

"See him go!" the boys on shore shouted.

Ben's friends helped him out, dripping, long before the other swimmers reached shore.

"These paddles can pull me through the water real fast," Ben panted. "But they take a lot of work, too." Ben took off his homemade paddles. "I'm tired out," he admitted.

This was only one of Ben's many experiments in the water. He remembered how hard he had had to work with the paddles. He decided to invent a way to go through the water with no work at all. He had the idea one day when he was flying a kite.

"I can use this kite for a sail to carry me across the pond," he told his friends.

The other boys looked doubtful, but they had found it wise to listen to Ben's ideas. Finally one of them said, "Prove it!"

Nothing made Ben so happy as to make an idea work. "All right," he said. "Hold my kite. But don't get the string tangled!"

The other boys looked on in surprise as Ben took off his clothes and dived into the water. "Give me the string," he said, holding up one hand for his kite string.

For a moment Ben lay floating on the water near shore. Then a stiff breeze caught his kite. It tugged at the string. And away Ben sailed, a satisfied grin on his face.

The other boys were so surprised they could not say a word.

"Hey!" Ben yelled. In the center of the pond, Ben had a sudden thought. "Will somebody please meet me on the other side — with my clothes?"

Laughing, Ben's friends picked up his clothes and carried them around the pond.

Another time Ben and a number of his friends were fishing for minnows at the edge of an inlet.

"Look at this big fellow!" one boy yelled as he held a squirming minnow by the tail. Just then the minnow flipped back into the pond. All of the boys reached into the water at once, but the minnow swam away.

"If this bank hadn't been so slippery, we'd

have had him," wailed one of Ben's friends.

The boys looked down at their legs. They were wet up to the knees!

"Jimminy! Will my ma scold me!" ... "*My* mother told me to stay away from here."

Ben could feel the water squishing in his shoes. He knew that his mother would not like his coming home again with wet feet. But he was deep in thought. If this bank weren't so trampled down —

"A wharf!" cried Ben. "We need a wharf. We could build one if we had some stones."

Then Ben remembered that they had passed a pile of stones on the way to the pond. The stones were for the foundation of a new house.

"Those stones back there! They're just what we need." Ben's gray eyes sparkled. Already he was planning how the wharf should be built. "We'll place the larger stones first. Then we'll fill in with smaller ones."

"But the workmen — " one of Ben's friends reminded him. "They won't let us."

"Oh, yes, the workmen." Ben pushed his cap back and rubbed his head. "We'll wait till they go home for supper." Ben saw the shadows the sun was beginning to cast over the water. "It won't be long."

The boys watched. When the workmen picked up their shovels and lunch pails and started home, Ben shouted, "Now!" The boys descended on the pile of stones like an army of ants.

"The biggest ones first," Ben directed. The boys found the larger stones heavy. It took two and three boys to roll them into position. But they worked hard. By the time it was dark they had moved all the stones to the water's edge and put them in place there.

"Now we have a good wharf," said Ben happily. "Now we can fish for minnows without sloshing in the muck." Tired and hungry, but happy, the boys trudged home.

"Will my mother ever be mad," one of the boys said. "All wet — and late again."

"You can tell her it won't happen again," Ben advised quickly.

But Ben was not thinking far enough ahead. The next morning the workmen found that their stones were gone. The boys' footprints led the men to the new wharf. The angry workmen soon traced "that Franklin boy," the ringleader of the group. He was told to round up his friends. Then the men found the fathers of the boys.

The fathers ordered their sons to move every stone back to where they had found it. While the boys worked, they talked of the lickings they would likely get. After the stones were moved back, Ben had to see his father.

"Why did you do it, son?" Mr. Franklin asked.

"We made a very good and useful wharf," Ben pointed out.

Ben's father was thoughtful for a moment. Then he said, "You must learn something, Benjamin. Nothing is really useful or good if it is gained by dishonest means. Remember that."

The words seemed to burn. Ben waited.

"That's all," said Ben's father. He turned to the fireplace, where a big kettle of tallow for candles was heating. Carefully he placed a wick in a mold. Then he ladled out the hot tallow. He filled several molds. As Ben watched, his father's words seemed to sink deeper and deeper in his mind: "Nothing is really useful or good if it is gained by dishonest means."

CHAPTER THREE

• CANDLESTICK MAKER •

Ben started to school when he was eight years old. After two years the teacher reported to Ben's father that Ben had failed in arithmetic. Ben could tell that his father was disappointed.

"Of all my seventeen children, I thought you might be the one to be a scholar," Mr. Franklin said a little sadly. "But perhaps it is just as well. Most scholars seem to have a hard time making a living. Instead of going to school you should be taught a trade."

Ben did not remember the time when he could not read. He had read *Pilgrim's Progress* and thought it exciting. He loved to read and write, but he did not like numbers.

"We shall try to choose a trade that you like," Ben's father said.

So Ben and his father began to visit different shops and factories in Boston. Ben watched the cobblers make shoes. He watched, amazed, as the blacksmith shaped red-hot metal before his blazing hearth, then made the metal into horseshoes and shod the horses. He visited the butcher and the baker. On his trips around the city with his father Ben learned much about all sorts of trades.

At last Ben's father asked, "Well, son, what trade do you like best?"

Ben did not know what to say.

"A workman should like his work," Mr. Franklin pointed out. "How would you like to go with your Uncle Benjamin's son?"

Ben had enjoyed watching the men in his cousin's cutlery factory. He had seen them shape the knives from white-hot metal, temper them in cold water, then hone them to glistening sharpness.

"Making knives was as interesting as any trade we saw," Ben finally answered. Then suddenly he asked, "Father, why can't I go to sea like my brother Joe? I'd like that better than anything!"

Josiah Franklin's face fell. It was as though the sun had been shining and suddenly a cloud had passed. Ben was sorry he had asked.

Patiently, Ben's father explained. "Life at sea is uncertain and dangerous. Your brother is away for months at a time. You are our youngest son. Your mother and I had hoped we could keep you near us."

And so Ben spent several weeks with his cousin, learning to be a knife-maker. Then the plan was given up. Josiah Franklin thought Ben's cousin wanted too much money to teach Ben the trade.

"Come home and learn candlemaking,"
Ben's father said. "Everybody needs candles.
You won't get rich at this trade but it is a
good one."

The days, the weeks, and the months
dragged by. Ben cut wicks. He brought in
wood needed for the big fire to melt the tallow. He poured the tallow into the candle
molds. And he cleaned the mess the tallow
drippings made on the floor. Ben hated the
smell of hot tallow grease. He hated cleaning
the mess. Every day he disliked more this
trade of candlemaking.

After two years Ben's father could tell that
his youngest son was not fitted to be a can-
dlemaker. One of the older Franklin boys,
James, had recently returned from England
where he had learned to be a printer. He
had brought a printing press back with him
and was going to go into the printing business in Boston.

"How would you like to work for James?"
Mr. Franklin asked Ben.

Ben did not know whether he would like
to work for James or not. And James was
not anxious to have Ben work for him. But
Josiah Franklin pointed out the advantages
for both.

"You could learn the printing trade as your brother's apprentice," he told Ben. To James he said, "You will be getting a smart boy and a good worker, when he has a mind to be. He is bookish and I have an idea he will take to the work." Then Mr. Franklin added, "You would be doing your mother and me a real service to occupy Ben in a way to take his mind off the sea."

Ben hesitated. He would have to sign papers saying he would work for James for nine years. That seemed like a long time. But Ben was eager to get away from candlemaking.

At last the agreements were made. Ben must work as apprentice for his brother until he was twenty-one. For his work Ben was to receive his meals, a room, and the opportunity to learn the printing trade.

CHAPTER FOUR

• PRINTER'S BOY •

Going to work in the printing shop of his brother James was like opening a door to a whole new world for Ben. He took part in all the work in the shop. He set the type in place, ran errands, and swept out the shop. Soon he became interested in writing.

In the printing shop Ben had a chance to borrow many books. Some he read at night and returned the next morning. He bought a few, traded a few. Always he was looking for more books to read.

Ben traded books with a friend, John Collins, who liked to read, too. The boys had many arguments about the books they read.

They liked to argue. Sometimes they argued for days on a subject.

About this time Ben made an important discovery in a book by Socrates. "I have been reasoning all wrong," he told his father. "Now I am trying a new way of arguing. And it works. I have quit saying 'This is so.' Instead I ask, 'Wouldn't it seem thus and so?' I never say *positively* or *undoubtedly*. Instead I say 'It would seem.' "

Ben's father smiled. "That is real wisdom, son."

Ben continued, "Do you know, Father, the other day I was arguing with John. Before he knew what was happening, he was arguing on *my side!*"

"I am glad you have discovered such valuable knowledge so young," Josiah Franklin said. "Only a wise person can learn from others."

Ben took more and more interest in studying. He even mastered arithmetic and then took up algebra and geometry. But his greatest interest was in writing.

One problem worried Ben. There were never enough hours for his studying, his reading, and his writing. Often he stayed up most of the night. Still he could not stretch his time far enough. So one day he suggested a plan to his brother James.

"Pay me half of what you pay the landlady for my board, and I will fix my own meals. If you do this, we can both save money."

James Franklin agreed. Ben was happy with the arrangement. A few slices of bread and a handful of raisins satisfied him at noon. When the others left the shop to eat, Ben sat down to read and study and write. He managed to save about half of the money James gave him for food. This he spent on books.

One day Ben had another idea. He was setting type for his brother's paper, the *New England Courant.*

"I can write better articles than this," Ben muttered. "People would like them better, too." That night in his room Ben wrote an article. He did not sign his name. He believed James would not print the article if he knew it was written by his youngest brother. So Ben thought of a name to use as author. The name was *Mrs. Silence Dogood.*

Ben finished his writing after midnight. Then he stole to the door of the printing shop and slipped the article underneath. Back in his attic room Ben went to sleep with a grin on his face.

What excitement his story caused in the shop the next morning!

"Who could have written this article?" James Franklin asked when he found the story. He called in his friends.

"It has wit. It is to the point. And it is

bound to stir up lots of comment," they told James.

Ben went about his work as though nothing had happened. It was a great thrill when his brother called him and said, "Here, boy, set this in type. We'll run it tomorrow."

Ben's article caused so much comment that he decided to write more. So Silence Dogood became a regular writer for the paper. She was supposed to be a poor widow. What she said about the news of the times was followed with great interest by the *Courant* readers. They liked her wisdom and her wit. Ben slipped the articles under the door at night.

"James thinks the Silence Dogood articles are clever," Ben muttered. "But he wouldn't, if he knew I wrote them."

As time went on, Ben and his brother got along worse instead of better.

Ben thought James was too bossy and treated him as a "slave."

James thought Ben was impudent and too independent. Sometimes he was so annoyed that he struck at his young brother.

Ben knew that, as his brother's apprentice, he was bound to do as he was told. He must also treat his master with respect. But the temptation to strike back in some way was too great.

One day, when Ben thought he had taken enough, he felt reckless. "You think you're smart, don't you?" he burst out. "Then tell me, if you can, who is Silence Dogood?"

James was startled at the tone of Ben's voice. "Who?" he demanded as though he dreaded to hear the answer.

"Me!" Ben blurted out defiantly.

Once the truth was known, that the mysterious, the wise, the witty Silence Dogood was the printer's boy, Ben Franklin, everyone was interested in Ben. The friends of James stopped to talk with his younger brother.

James was angry at the trick Ben had played. It became hard for Ben to please him with anything.

Ben thought he could bear it no longer. Then something happened to separate the brothers. James was put in prison because of some articles he had published. The *Courant* had dared to criticize the Assembly, which governed the colony.

Ben felt a little guilty. He knew the critical opinions of Silence Dogood had not helped.

James was in prison for a month. During that time Ben managed the *Courant*. Ben defended James hotly in the paper. When James was released from prison, the brothers were better friends. But soon the old problems arose again.

James said Ben had too much "crust," "felt his oats," and was too "sassy." One day James struck Ben harder than usual.

Ben knew that was a master's privilege.

But he was now seventeen years old. He decided he would stand it no longer. That night he told his friend, John Collins, "I'm going to run away."

"But you are bound to your brother until you are twenty-one. He'll catch you and bring you back," John pointed out.

"No, I'll escape. Will you help me?"

Ben was not afraid. He believed he could get a good job in a printing shop in some other city. He had only one regret about leaving Boston. He hated to go without telling his parents good-by. Yet if he did, he knew that his father would stop him.

CHAPTER FIVE

• RUNAWAY •

Good-by, Boston! An early morning fog rolled from the sea into Boston Harbor. It was so thick that Benjamin Franklin, runaway printer's boy, could hardly see the wharf. He looked back from the little ship he had slipped aboard during the night.

John Collins had arranged everything. He had helped sell Ben's books to get money for the trip. And he had seen the captain about taking Ben to New York.

Soon the little ship glided away into the fog. Ben thought about the sea voyages he used to plan. Someway, he didn't know how, he had lost most of his interest in the sea.

The ship took three days to go from Boston to New York. And when Ben arrived in New York he met with disappointment. William Bradford, who had the only printing shop in the city, had no work for him.

"I advise you to go to Philadelphia," the kind old man told Ben. "My son, Andrew, has a printing shop there. And it happens that he needs a man. I'll give you a letter to him."

In a few hours Ben was back on the water, on his way to Philadelphia. Soon the wind began to blow. It grew stronger. The little ship was in the midst of a squall. It scudded along. The wind whipped it first one way, then the other. The waves swished and rolled.

Suddenly a gust of wind whipped the boat around. It tore the sails from the mast. A piece of wet sail slapped Ben in the face.

Ben shuddered. Would the storm never end? How much more could the little ship stand?

"She blows big!" A friendly Hollander from New York nudged Ben's arm.

The next moment a wave seemed to swallow the ship. It rose at last, dripping from bow to stern. Then Ben heard a terrified scream. The man who had been standing beside him had been washed overboard and was struggling in the water.

Ben had no time to think. He leaned over the side, reached as far as he could, and grabbed. Ben's hand touched the man's head. His fingers tightened on the man's hair.

"Help!" Ben shouted above the noise of the storm.

The captain rushed to Ben's aid. The two of them dragged the man on board.

"You save life!" the man sputtered. Then he began to pull uneasily at something in his pocket.

Ben wondered what the man had. Was it a bag of money?

Finally the man pulled the object free. He held it up for Ben to see.

"A book! A copy of my old favorite — *Pilgrim's Progress!*" Ben exclaimed.

"You fix?" the Hollander asked.

"You mean you want me to dry it?" Ben wiped the book carefully with his sleeve. He had never before seen such a beautiful book.

It was printed in Dutch on fine paper. Beautiful pictures decorated the pages.

The boat heaved and pitched. But for a few minutes Ben and the man he had saved were thinking only of a book. The Hollander was anxious to learn if the water would hurt his treasure. And Ben was marveling at the workmanship of the book.

At last the Hollander was satisfied that the book was not ruined. He rubbed his eyes sleepily and stumbled toward the hatchway. There, where goods were loaded into the ship, he would be partly under cover. The man lay down in his wet clothes. Ben noticed that he soon was fast asleep.

The storm drove the small ship close to shore. But there was no place to land.

"We'll have to drop anchor and wait the storm out," the captain said. So Ben and the captain lay down in the hatchway beside the wet Hollander.

The hatchway offered little protection from the cold wind. Cold spray beat over the ship's bow and leaked through. The Hollander, sleeping beside Ben, snored loudly. Ben thought that he never before had spent such a miserable night.

"Shiver my timbers, if we're not as wet as the one who fell in!" exclaimed the captain in disgust.

Miserable as he was, Ben had to laugh. "I used to think I wanted to go to sea," he admitted. "But if I had any such idea left, this night has washed it away!"

The next morning the storm calmed. But the crippled ship took most of the day to reach Amboy, across the bay from New York. Ben had spent thirty hours, without food, on storm-tossed waters. He decided he would walk across land to Burlington, a town on the Delaware River. There he would catch a boat down the river to Philadelphia.

The next morning Ben started his long walk to Burlington, fifty miles away. Rain was pouring down. Ben was drenched to the skin. But he kept on walking.

At noon he stopped to rest at a poor inn. People looked at him suspiciously. He knew they thought he was a runaway servant.

Ben was uneasy. He was lonely, and he was homesick. He began to wish that he had never run away.

CHAPTER SIX

• CITY OF BROTHERLY LOVE •

Ben missed the regular boat from Burlington to Philadelphia. Some men in a rowboat offered him a ride down the river. Ben helped with the rowing. He was tired, dirty, and hungry when the boat tied up at Market Street wharf in Philadelphia. It was early on a Sunday morning. The little colonial city was just beginning to awaken.

Ben offered to pay the owner of the boat.

"No, no. Keep your money," the owner said. "You earned your trip by rowing!"

Ben insisted on paying. He gave the man all the small change in his pocket. He had only a single dollar left.

"I didn't pay too much for *that* whistle," Ben told himself. Ever since the time, years before, when he had learned his first lesson in thrift, he had called wasting money paying too much for a *whistle*.

"A man is sometimes more generous when he has little money than when he has plenty," Ben said. "Perhaps because he fears people will think he has but little."

Ben was hungry. He walked up the street, searching for food. At a bakeshop he asked for three biscuits. Three biscuits like those he was used to in Boston would satisfy him.

"Biscuits? I must tell thee I do not have any such thing," the baker said, speaking in the manner of the Quakers.

"A three-penny loaf of bread then."

"Thee must come from away," the baker said, "for thee art asking for something else I do not have."

At last Ben asked, "Then will you give me

three pennies' worth of bread of any sort?"

The baker handed Ben three big rolls.

Ben was surprised to get so much. For a moment he juggled the three big rolls of bread like a magician. Then he managed to tuck one under one arm and another under his other arm. Hungrily he bit into the third.

He was eager to see more of Philadelphia so as he ate his roll Ben walked along Market Street. Passing a doorway he saw a pretty girl watching him. Her expression of surprise changed to a merry giggle.

Suddenly Ben realized how funny he must look. The joke was on him. And he, too, laughed. Everybody seems so friendly, thought Ben. No wonder Philadelphia is called the City of Brotherly Love.

After Ben had eaten one of the big rolls he was no longer hungry. He gave the other two rolls to a woman and her child.

Going back up Market Street Ben met

many people dressed for church. He followed
them to the meeting house of the Quakers,
known as the Friends. He had never before
been in a Quaker church.

The women sat on one side of the room.

The men sat on the other side. Ben followed the men and found a seat. He was very tired. Soon he was sound asleep. He did not know how long he slept. When the meeting was over, a man tapped him on the shoulder. Ben awakened with a start.

Back on the street he asked the way to a place to stay. A man directed him to the Crooked Billet on Water Street.

Ben thought he never before had been so tired. After dinner he went to his room. He fell on the bed and went to sleep in his clothes. And after supper he went back to bed and slept until morning.

Ben awoke refreshed. He cleaned up. Then he went to look for Andrew Bradford.

When Ben walked into Bradford's printing shop his eyes lit up. There was old Mr. Bradford sitting in his son's office! He had come from New York on horseback and had arrived before Ben.

The younger Bradford no longer needed a printer. He had already hired one. "Why don't you go to see Mr. Keimer?" he suggested. "He is opening a new shop." Then he kindly offered Ben a place to stay. He also promised Ben extra work when he had it. The father offered to take Ben to Mr. Keimer.

"Neighbor, I've brought you a fine young printer," old Mr. Bradford said.

Ben listened to the two men with interest. Mr. Keimer did not know who Mr. Bradford was. Thinking that he was a well-meaning resident of Philadelphia, Keimer told all his plans for the future. In time, he said he would get all of Andrew Bradford's business.

Slyly the old man winked at Ben. Then he asked all sorts of questions. When he had heard enough, he left Ben with Keimer.

"That was Andrew Bradford's father," Ben told Keimer.

"It *was?* Horrors!" Keimer was embarrassed at all he had said. "Well, young man, let's see what you can do." He handed Ben a small tray for arranging type, called a composing stick.

Quickly, skillfully, Ben set several lines of type. He put blank pieces of metal between the words for spaces. He put blank metal strips, called slugs, between the lines. When he had finished, the words fitted perfectly. The lines were neat and even. Keimer whistled. This boy was a good printer!

"I can see you've had good experience," he said. "I'll call on you when I need help."

Ben had noticed several things about the shop. The press was old and broken down. He also saw that Keimer had been setting type himself.

"How long have you had this press? How much type do you have? Do you not have a copy of the work you are setting?" Ben asked.

Keimer admitted that he had just recently

bought the press and had never tried to use it. He had only enough letters of type for the poem he was setting. And he was setting type "straight from his head." This meant that he did not write down the words first.

Ben frowned. He had been trained that a good printer should see the words he was setting in type. In this way he could avoid many mistakes.

Ben could tell that Keimer did not know much about presses. "Want me to check your press and get her ready to go?" Ben asked.

"Would you? I've been busy," Keimer answered. Ben could see his eagerness.

Ben took off his jacket and rolled up his sleeves. "It's good to be back at a press," he said. "Now, a bolt here will fix this loose place." Soon he was whistling a merry tune. "A press should sit firm and level." He found some pieces of wood and slid them under one side of the old frame on the uneven floor.

"And I wouldn't be surprised if this right side bears down too heavily." Ben slowly closed down the top part of the press. He carefully watched the space narrow between it and the frame where the type lay. "Just as I thought," he said. "The right side prints too heavy to read. The left side prints too light to show."

Ben worked for several hours. At last he had the old press working properly.

For a while Ben worked part of the time for Keimer and part of the time for Bradford. Between the two jobs he kept busy.

Keimer did not like it that Ben lived with Bradford, so Ben decided to look for another place to stay. He was directed to a Mr. Read's house. Ben climbed the steps from the street and knocked. A pretty girl came to the door.

"Oh, you're the — " Ben and the girl each spoke the same words in surprise. Then they both began to laugh.

"Yes. I'm the one with the rolls. And you're the girl who laughed at me!" Ben loved the way the laughter seemed to bubble from her lips.

Ben knew he looked quite different than he had the morning of his arrival in Philadelphia. His good suit was clean and pressed. The ruffles on his white shirt were starched and clean. The admiring eyes of the girl told Ben that she thought him handsome.

Ben found that the girl's name was Deborah Read. "But everybody always calls me Debbie," she explained.

Happily Ben moved his trunk into a room at the Reads' house. He knew that he and Debbie already were well on the way to becoming good friends.

CHAPTER SEVEN

• "ON THY SELF DEPEND" •

Ben made friends easily. He was full of fun. He loved people. And he was interested in what they thought and in what they did. With Ben's help, Keimer soon had enough work to keep his printing shop busy.

Meanwhile Ben's opinion of Philadelphia printers dropped lower and lower. Keimer was not bad at composing, or at writing. But he knew little about printing. Bradford was not bad at handling the presses. But he knew little about writing, grammar, and spelling. Neither shop turned out fine, clean work, free of mistakes. Ben was not proud of it.

One day Ben and Keimer were setting type

when two well-dressed men came to the door.

"That is Sir William Keith, governor of the province," Keimer whispered. He straightened his apron and rushed excitedly to the door.

The colonies were still ruled by the mother country — Great Britain. The governors of the provinces were appointed by the king of England. A printing job from the governor would pay well!

Keimer greeted the governor expectantly.

Governor Keith brushed him aside. "Is Mr. Benjamin Franklin to be found here? I desire to see him," he stated importantly.

The governor greeted Ben warmly. "I have heard through your brother-in-law, Robert Holmes, that you are a fine printer. The other day, he showed me a letter of yours. I was quite impressed."

Ben remembered he had written Robert a letter explaining why he had run away.

Sir Keith introduced the man with him as Colonel French and graciously invited Ben to have dinner with them.

Ben saw that Keimer was disturbed and angry. He could not help enjoying Keimer's jealousy almost as much as the governor's pleasant talk. He accepted Governor Keith's invitation gladly.

At dinner the governor told Ben that he wished to set him up in business as a printer. "Colonel French and I would give you all of our official printing jobs," he said. "With a little help from your father, success is sure."

Ben was pleased and excited with Governor Keith's suggestion. "But I doubt if my father would put money in the business," Ben said. "Father is a thrifty and cautious man. And he is not rich."

Governor Keith was not to be stopped in his idea. "Philadelphia hasn't a single good printer!" he exclaimed. "I will write to your father. This can mean your whole future."

Ben agreed to take the governor's letter to his father. He would try to get his help in starting a printing shop in Philadelphia. Ben also agreed not to tell Keimer of the plan.

In April, 1724, Ben took a boat for Boston. Keimer thought he was going on a short trip to visit friends. It had been seven months since Ben had seen his family. It seemed more like seven years!

Ben walked to his old home from the Boston wharf. He noticed that the blue ball was still hanging over the door. The door was closed, for a chill spring breeze was blowing in from the harbor. Ben hesitated. He was eager to see his family, but he wondered how they would receive him. At last he opened the door. There was the family sitting around the wide open fireplace. His father was reading by candlelight. Ben noticed that his mother looked older, and a little sad.

When she saw who was there, her face lit up. "Benjamin!" she cried. She kissed and hugged him, then wiped away some tears.

"You're looking fine, son!" Ben's father put his arm around him.

It was a gay and happy evening in the Franklin home. They talked of the affairs of the colonies, politics, and the happenings in Boston. Ben's father could discuss these subjects with wisdom and understanding.

Ben had always admired his father. Now, sitting in the warmth of his old home, Ben thought: Father is a great man. He is the greatest man I have ever known.

Finally Josiah Franklin got out his fiddle, as he often had done when Ben was a child. It was the same home, Ben realized happily, that he had remembered with longing. And when his father began to sing in his clear voice, Ben had to swallow hard.

While he was at home Ben went to visit

James in his printing shop. James looked his younger brother over from head to foot. Then, without a word, he turned back to his work. The men in the shop gathered around Ben.

"How is Philadelphia?" . . . "Is there plenty of work?" . . . "How is the pay?" they asked eagerly.

Ben was dressed better than he had ever been in Boston. He had a watch, something few men could afford. He pulled a handful of silver coins from his pocket. The men were surprised to see the silver. They were used to paper money in Boston. Ben put several coins on the table. "A treat for the office," he said a little grandly.

Ben knew that his visit made James angry. "I shouldn't have done it," Ben admitted to his mother later. "But I guess I was still smarting from the last licking he gave me. I am not sorry."

Mr. Franklin studied the letter Ben

brought from Governor Keith. He seemed a little surprised that a stranger would recommend his own son to him.

After several days he gave his decision. "I am pleased with the governor's good opinion of you, Benjamin. But I think the man must have little judgment to entrust such an undertaking to one so young. You have three years yet until you reach manhood. Go back to Philadelphia, son. Work hard. Save your money. By the time you are one and twenty you may have almost enough money to buy your own presses. If you do, I will help you."

Ben nodded.

"And one more thing, Benjamin," Mr. Franklin went on. "Treat people with respect. You are too fond of fun! Try to avoid saying and writing things that will likely get you into trouble."

Ben grinned. He was not unhappy about

his father's decision. And before long he was convinced that his father was right.

Josiah Franklin wrote a polite letter for Ben to take to Sir William Keith. In it he told the governor that he thought his son too young for the responsibilities suggested.

"Sometimes younger people have better judgment than older ones," Sir William said. "If your father will not furnish the money, I will. Make out a list of the things you need, Ben. Then you shall go to England to buy your press. I am sure you will be a great success as a printer. And I am determined to get a good printer in Philadelphia!"

A ship sailed from Boston to England once a year. The ship was called the *Annis*. During the months Ben waited for the ship, Sir William promised time and again to give Ben money. But every time Ben went for it, it was not ready. Then Sir William promised to send the money on board the ship.

Ben sailed on the *Annis*. Too late, he realized that Sir William Keith had made promises he would never keep.

So, on Christmas Eve, 1724, Benjamin Franklin landed in England with almost no money. He was completely on his own in a strange land.

Ben thought back over the last few months. He was surprised and hurt at the treatment he had received from a friend. Pulling a piece of paper from his pocket he wrote:
"In things of moment, on thy self depend,
 Nor trust too far thy Servant or thy Friend."

Ben looked critically at what he had written. "I'll write some more on this someday," he said. Then he grinned. Coming toward him were Mr. Denham, a Quaker merchant, and another good friend he had made on the trip.

CHAPTER EIGHT

• ONE AND TWENTY •

Ben spent a year and a half in England and became a fine printer. When he returned to Philadelphia, Mr. Denham made him a partner in his store. After an illness Mr. Denham died. Ben was sick, too. When he recovered, he took a job again with Keimer.

Keimer had five workmen. He paid them little, because they were unskilled. He hired Ben as manager of the shop.

Patiently Ben tried to teach the untrained men the art of printing. As the others learned more from Ben, Keimer felt less and less need of Ben's help. His treatment of Ben became more and more unpleasant. When he paid Ben he even told him he thought the pay was too much. Ben believed that Keimer was planning to let the men who worked for less money do his work. He expected that Keimer would find an excuse to let him go.

One day Ben heard a loud noise in the street outside. He left his work to look out the window. Keimer was in the street below. Looking up, he saw Ben.

"At the wages you're getting I should think you could pay better attention to your work," Keimer shouted.

Here at last, thought Ben, is the quarrel Keimer has wanted to pick! Ben had not thought that Keimer would choose this way — insulting him in public!

Keimer's shouting had attracted an interested crowd. Ben could see from their eager faces that they hoped for a fight. He tried to control his temper.

"Are you trying to embarrass me in public?" he asked Keimer. "If so, you are embarrassing yourself as well."

The crowd laughed. "That's right, Ben! Tell him," someone yelled.

Keimer came inside and continued the argument. "You're fired," he finally shouted. "I only wish I did not have to give you three months notice!"

By this time Ben was furious. "It isn't necessary to give me notice," he said. He grabbed his hat and left.

That evening Hugh Meredith, one of the workmen Ben had been teaching, came to Ben's room. He brought the things Ben had not stopped to take.

"I don't want to stay with Keimer if you don't," Hugh said. "You've taught me everything I know about printing. At the rate Keimer is going, he won't stay open long. He can't keep accounts straight. Half the time he doesn't have any record of the bills he should collect. And he's in debt to almost everybody."

Ben nodded. "I know of Keimer's sloppy ways," he said. "But what would you do if you didn't work for Keimer?"

"Father admires you very much," Meredith told Ben. "I've already talked to him about setting us up in business together. My time at Keimer's will be up in a few months."

"But I don't have money to pay my share of a printing business," Ben said.

"I wouldn't expect it," Hugh replied quickly. "I know that I'll never be much good at printing. I'm willing to match the money with your skill and we will share equally in the profits. I believe Father will furnish me the money."

Mr. Meredith, a prosperous farmer, was in Philadelphia that evening. Ben and Hugh went to see him. Mr. Meredith was pleased with the plan. He thought Ben would be a good influence on his son. He asked Ben to make a list of everything needed for a printing shop. He promised to have his merchant send to England for this equipment.

After a few days Keimer wrote Ben a note. "Old friends should not part over a few hasty words," the note said. Mr. Keimer asked Ben to return to his job.

Ben found that Keimer had an opportunity to print paper money for the government. The job would take a printer of great skill. Ben was the only one Keimer knew who could do the work. This, Ben believed, was why Keimer was asking him to come back.

Ben decided to go back to work for Keimer. He made fine engravings and copperplates for the paper money. He met many new people and made many friends in government positions.

Soon after this job was done, the new press and type Hugh's father had ordered arrived

from England. Ben and Hugh rented a house and set up the press.

Many people believed Franklin would fail. "There is not enough business in Philadelphia for three shops," they said. But friends began to bring printing jobs to the new shop.

Ben worked hard. One of his first jobs was printing forty pages of Quaker history. Ben was determined to set a whole page of type every day. Often he had to work into the night to do this. One evening, by working especially hard, he set two pages. Just as he finished, he dropped the form, and the type fell out.

"Two pages reduced to pi — just a mess of type," he said. Patiently, wearily, he set to work resetting the pages. He did not stop until he had finished.

People passing Franklin's shop late at night often noticed him at work. "The industry of that Franklin is superior to anything I ever saw of the kind," one man, a doctor, said. "I see him still at work when I go home from my club, and he is at work again before his neighbors are out of bed."

CHAPTER NINE

• BEN TAKES A WIFE •

"He that would thrive must ask his wife," Ben said softly. "That's a good old English proverb. Do you think I can afford a new book, wife?" Ben looked admiringly at his bride. In September, 1730, he had married Debbie Read, the girl who had laughed at him on his first morning in Philadelphia.

"How did I ever get along without you?" Ben asked teasingly. "You keep my shirts starched white. You work hard in the shop. You help me with my books. And you save my money. Soon I'll have my debts all paid."

Debbie smiled. "I have to work hard to keep up with my ambitious husband."

Ben had bought the Merediths' interest in the printing shop. Two of his friends, William Coleman and Robert Grace, had loaned him the money. At last, in 1729, he had his own shop.

Ben worked hard from early morning until late at night. Often he wheeled his paper to the shop in a wheelbarrow. He never stopped in the taverns. He never went hunting or fishing. His only recreation was reading.

He had many friends who also liked to read. They formed a group which they called the Junto. The members met once a week to discuss their books, politics, and news.

"We can all bring our books to one place," Ben suggested. "In that way each of us can have the advantages of reading many books."

The plan worked so well that Ben had another idea. "Let us invite others to join us. Then we can have a bigger library."

Members of the Junto were enthusiastic.

They asked their friends to contribute and to promise to pay a certain amount each year for fifty years. Fifty citizens of Philadelphia agreed to give to a library fund. This was the beginning of the Philadelphia Public Library — the first public library in the world. Men from other cities soon learned about the Philadelphia Library and copied the plan.

Ben's printing business grew. However, Bradford still controlled much of the printing business in Philadelphia. He published the record of the votes and the laws for the Assembly. Ben thought that Bradford did very poor work. His spelling was bad and the printing smeared.

Ben reprinted one of the speeches given in the Assembly. He took pride in perfect spelling and beautiful, clean type. When he had finished, he gave copies to each member of the Assembly. The members compared Ben's work with Bradford's. Then they voted to give all the printing work of the Assembly to Franklin.

When a bill to print more paper money was passed, Franklin was given the job of printing the new money. The job paid him well.

Business in the Benjamin Franklin Printing Company grew fast, and Franklin was rapidly paying off his debts. He had a chance to buy Keimer's newspaper cheaply. Now he had a newspaper of his own. Ever since he had been in his brother's shop in Boston he had wanted this. Franklin published his paper, *The Pennsylvania Gazette*, once a week. This paper was the beginning of *The Saturday Evening Post*.

Along with his business, Franklin's family grew. He became the father of two sons, William and Francis, whom he called Franky.

Debbie managed carefully. Besides working in the shop and in the home she bought old rags which were sold for making paper.

Many families in Philadelphia had expensive china and silver. They sent to England for fine clothes and furniture. The Franklins had none of these things. They lived plainly. Ben disliked waste and extravagance. He believed that every man should save a part of what he earned. He wore his clothes a long time. The family ate from cheap earthen dishes made in America. They used pewter spoons.

One morning when Franklin sat down to breakfast he noticed a fine china bowl on the table. At his place was a silver spoon.

"What does this mean?" he said in annoyance. "Has my wife turned into a spendthrift overnight?"

Mrs. Franklin calmly tied a napkin around William's neck. Then she sat down across from her husband with Franky in her arms. She fed a spoonful of mush to the baby before she spoke.

"I have no excuses to make. I just think *my* husband deserves a china bowl and a silver spoon as much as any of his neighbors!"

For once, Benjamin Franklin had nothing to say.

As the years passed, many fine things were added to the home. Franklin wanted the best for his sons. When Franky was two and William four, Ben put an ad in his *Gazette*.

"Wanted: A servant who is a scholar and can teach children reading, writing, and arithmetic."

CHAPTER TEN

• POOR RICHARD •

"Early to bed and early to rise makes a man healthy, wealthy, and wise." Benjamin Franklin chuckled. "I know the readers of my almanac will like that."

Debbie looked up from her sewing. "You mean everybody in all the colonies, because everybody reads your almanac."

The almanac that Franklin had started was a calendar booklet giving the date and weather forecast. It told about the sun, moon, and stars. To this, Franklin added many clever sayings. He called the booklet *Poor Richard's Almanac*.

The colonists had few books and newspapers to read. On cold winter evenings they read the almanac by candlelight for amusement. In the spring they planted their crops according to the almanac suggestions. In the summer and fall they tended and reaped their crops after studying the almanac.

Debbie smiled proudly. "Everybody reads your newspaper, too, Mr. Franklin. Remember the ad you put in the paper last year when William lost his pony? You could hardly get any work done for weeks because everybody was asking about the pony."

Franklin grinned as he thought of the ad: "A small bay mare . . . She, being but little and barefooted, cannot have gone far. If any of the town boys find her and bring her back, they shall, for their trouble, have the liberty to ride her when they please."

"A little barefooted pony," said Debbie, "had everybody in Philadelphia looking for her."

"Was that a whole year ago?" asked Franklin. "It seems more like a month."

Debbie nodded. "William is thirteen now."

Suddenly, as he often did, Franklin thought of little Franky, the son they had lost with smallpox when he was only four. That had been the greatest sadness of his life.

Franklin looked down in the cradle near the fireplace. He saw that the baby was awake and he stooped over to pick her up.

Baby Sally, named for her aunt, gurgled and pulled at Franklin's white wig. Franklin reached up and pulled the wig off. "Never did like these things — "

"Now that you are a member of the General Assembly, besides being city postmaster, and the most popular man in Philadelphia, it is fitting that you dress up a little," Debbie reminded her husband. "Mr. Franklin — " Debbie folded her arms — "did you ever stop to think of all the things you're working on?"

"I guess I do have a lot of irons in the fire." Franklin grinned. "The night watch is organized now and working fine." He spoke of the only police protection of those times. "And now that fire protection is organized we haven't had a big fire for some time." The first fire department in history was also one of Franklin's great Philadelphia projects. "And we have some militia of our own in case we're invaded by a foreign country."

Debbie looked at her husband proudly.

"And now I'd like to work on getting some means of educating our young people. . . . I have it. The Junto!" Franklin was speaking more to himself than to his wife as he rocked his youngest. The power of the Junto organization had grown. Each member had organized other groups throughout Philadelphia. The groups had great influence. The Junto, Franklin was thinking, would be helpful in organizing schools and colleges.

"It has been such a cold winter!" Debbie's voice broke in on her husband's thoughts. She got up and poked the logs in the big fireplace. The sparks popped out as she put on more logs. Soon the fire was blazing. Still the winter wind seemed to sweep in around the door and windows. Debbie drew her shawl close around her.

"All the heat seems to go up the chimney," Franklin said, half to himself.

Suddenly he jumped up. "Here, take the baby. I'm going to start work on a metal fireplace. It will take in fresh air, warm it, and send it out to warm the room."

Franklin sat down at the table. He picked up a quill pen made from a stiff feather. He dipped the pen into a bottle of ink. Then with fine, even lines he drew a picture.

Franklin went to Robert Grace, who owned a furnace for making iron products. Grace carefully followed Franklin's directions. In

1742, Franklin's metal, open-front stove was finished.

The stove was a great success. Franklin wrote a pamphlet on the "New-Invented Pennsylvanian Fire-Place." Soon many wanted one of Franklin's stoves. The governor offered Franklin a patent so that no one else could make the stoves. "You can soon be a very rich man," he told Franklin.

Franklin refused the patent. "I believe that all inventions should be freely given for the benefit of all of mankind," Franklin told the governor. "I am going to let Robert Grace make my stoves. He can make them quickly and cheaply in his iron furnace."

Franklin set up several printing shops in other cities. After he made a fair profit, he gave the managers the chance to buy. In this way he helped a number of people to get started in the printing business.

Franklin had a good income from his printing business, his newspaper, and his almanac. He felt, at last, that he could hire more helpers and do some of the things he wished.

He made a trip to Boston. He stopped at Newport, where James had moved his shop. At last, the brothers became good friends.

When he returned to Philadelphia, Franklin took up the study of French, Italian, Spanish, then Latin. He believed that Latin was the hardest language and should be studied after the others, not before them.

One day a doctor came to visit Franklin. His name was Dr. Thomas Bond.

"There's no such thing as carrying through a public-spirited project without your help, Mr. Franklin." Dr. Bond spoke seriously. "Everybody we ask says, 'Have you talked to Franklin about this? What does he think?'" Then the doctor added, "The plan will fail unless you help us!"

Benjamin Franklin smiled. "You may tell

everyone that you have talked with Franklin and that he is enthusiastic about a hospital! In fact, I am going to help you."

Franklin's eyes twinkled. "This is one of the times I am glad I can do a little scribbling. The first thing I am going to do is write some articles for my newspaper. This is a new idea. And so we must tell the people about it."

Franklin wrote many articles about Dr. Bond's plan for a hospital. At last, through his efforts, a fine hospital was built — the first one in America.

Through Franklin's efforts, too, the streets of Philadelphia were paved. Then other cities followed Philadelphia's good example.

"Molehills if often heaped, to mountains rise," Franklin wrote in his almanac. He might have been thinking of the way many of his hobbies grew into great inventions and improvements.

CHAPTER ELEVEN

• FLYING A KITE •

In 1746, when Franklin was visiting in Boston, he saw electrical experiments performed. What is electricity, he wondered? He bought some equipment and began to experiment.

Rubbing the fur of his cat, he saw the electric sparks. Standing out in a storm, he felt the charge in the air when lightning came close. He believed lightning was electricity and he determined to find out.

Franklin had noticed that many tall buildings and houses were struck by lightning. Some of them were burned to the ground.

"If I could only prove that lightning is electricity," Franklin said again and again. "Trees, church spires, and ship masts — tall, pointed objects — seem to attract the lightning."

At last he decided he would try a new experiment. He would see if he could attract lightning from a cloud.

"I will attach a sharp metal rod to the new church spire," Franklin said. "I will see if I can draw the electricity from lightning in a storm. I will run the rod into the ground so that the electricity can be carried from the point into the ground." Franklin wrote to scientists in France about his plan.

The church spire was slow in being built. Franklin grew impatient. "Perhaps I can get something else into the sky during a storm," he said to himself. Then his face broke into a smile. "Why, a kite!" he said. "A good kite!" He remembered the kite he had sent into the air many years before, the kite that had carried him sailing across the pond.

He explained his idea to his son, William, who was now a young man. "We usually have a strong wind during a storm," Franklin said. "I'll try sending a kite directly up into a cloud."

"Won't it be dangerous?" William asked. He was not enthusiastic but agreed to help.

Franklin waited for several weeks for a thunderstorm. Then one afternoon in June, 1752, he hurried to the window of his home. Dark clouds were piling up in the sky. In the distance bright lightning flashed. It seemed to leap from both sky and earth and join in a continuous chain. The thunder boomed like a cannon, then rumbled away.

"Hurry, William! I'll need your help!" Franklin shouted excitedly. "I think the clouds are coming close enough to try my electrical experiment."

The air was warm and sultry. "I hope no

one sees us," William said. He did not share his father's excitement.

Franklin brought out a kite he had made. He had crossed light pieces of cedar wood for a frame, and tacked to it a large silk handkerchief. At the top of the kite he had put a piece of wire, filed to a point.

The wind before the storm blew Franklin's long hair over his face. It flapped at his coat-tails, and it almost tore the kite from him.

Franklin and his son headed for a shed out in an open field. The dark cloud had risen higher.

"We will loose the kite from the doorway of this shed and fly it right up into that cloud!" Franklin exclaimed. "First I will put this little piece of silk ribbon on the end of the string. It will not soak up rain as quickly as cotton."

The kite tugged at its string. Its tail, with pieces of cloth tied to it, lashed back and

forth. The strong wind carried the kite up and up. The rumbling thunder grew louder, and louder. Suddenly there was a sharp crack and the sky lit up.

"Look at the string!" William shouted.

In the flash of bright light Franklin saw tiny loose fibers of the string standing straight out.

"Quick! A piece of metal. Metal attracts electricity. It will help us tell if we have electricity! Here, hold the string for me, William." Franklin felt in his pocket. A moment later he tied a key where the cotton string joined the silk ribbon.

Impatiently he waited. He touched the key several times but he could feel no spark or charge. "There *was* electricity," said Franklin. "The string showed there was."

Another flash of lightning ripped the air.

The cloud let forth a torrent of rain. This time lively sparks crackled from the key!

They jumped out to meet Franklin's fingers. When he touched the key he felt a sharp tingling.

"It is electricity!" shouted Franklin. He felt the string and found it wet. "Wet objects must carry electricity better than dry objects," he reasoned. "That is why we got no sparks before the rain, when the string was dry.

When the storm was over, Franklin and his son trudged back to the house.

"Was the experiment successful?" Debbie asked.

"Of course it was." Sally flung her curls back and put her arms around her father. "My papa is always successful."

Franklin smiled. But he was thinking of other things. "I am going to put a metal rod — a tall rod — on top of our house. It will point up into the air. I will run the rod straight down through the house by the stairway. And down into the earth below. The rod will carry the lightning into the ground so it will not strike the house."

"Benjamin Franklin! You'll kill yourself and have us all killed if you don't stop fooling with heavenly fire," Debbie objected.

In spite of Debbie's objections, Franklin built his rod. He attached it to the top of the chimney, letting the rod extend about nine feet above the chimney. At the foot of the rod he attached a wire. Where the wire touched the house he placed it in a glass tube. He brought the wire down along the stairway in the center of the house. He attached the wire to a metal pump which extended into the earth. Thus his lightning rod was safely grounded.

On the stairway, beside his bedroom door, Franklin divided the wire into two parts. He separated the parts about six inches and placed a little bell on each part. Between the two parts he hung a little brass ball by a silk thread. During thunderstorms the little ball played on the string and struck the bells so that they could be heard all over the house.

One stormy night Franklin heard a terrible cracking noise in the hall. He jumped out of bed and rushed to his door. White fire was passing in a continuous stream between the bells. The metal ball stood straight out on its silken string. The entire hall seemed ablaze with a white light.

The other members of the family burst into the hall. William and Sally rubbed their eyes in the glare. "Oh, Ben, whatever have you done?" shrieked Debbie in fright.

Franklin, still in his nightshirt, watched in awe. He had brought the electricity from a storm cloud right into the house!

"Why, it's as bright as sunshine," he said softly. "Anyone could see to pick up a pin."

Soon many other people placed rods on

their buildings. Franklin became known as the inventor of the lightning rod.

Franklin wrote to other scientists about his experiments. He also wrote about them in his famous almanac. He had to invent many new words to describe his work with electricity. Before long other scientists were using his words: battery, charged, uncharged, armature, conductor, discharge, electrical fire, electrical shock, electrician, electrify, and many others. What Franklin wrote was translated into foreign languages.

His experiments in electricity became known in many parts of the world. Harvard College and Yale University gave him honorary degrees. The Royal Society in London, England, sent him a gold medal and later elected him as a member. The King of France praised him as a great man, and people everywhere began to call him the great Doctor Franklin.

CHAPTER TWELVE

• PEACEMAKER •

"The Indians! Papa, are they going to make war?"

"I don't know, Sally," Benjamin Franklin answered his daughter. "We're going to try to keep them from making war."

"I declare, Ben," Debbie spoke sadly, "I thought at last you were going to settle down. Now you go off to meet the Indians. Goodness knows what for."

Franklin placed the warm scarf Debbie had knitted for him in the top of his knapsack. Then he buckled the top securely. He and two other members of the Assembly had been appointed as commissioners to meet the

Indians at Carlisle. This was a new settlement in wild country in western Pennsylvania. Franklin would rather have stayed at home. He wanted to continue his experiments in electricity. The trip would take several days of hard riding on horseback. But Franklin believed that it was every man's duty to serve the public. He never refused a public office or appointment.

On September 26, 1753, the commissioners reached Carlisle where about a hundred Indians — chiefs, braves, squaws, and papooses — made camp outside the settlement.

Ceremonies with the Indians dragged on for days, and the white men grew impatient. "Let's give them gifts and go back," one of the men suggested. "The Indians just want a bribe of gifts to keep peace."

Franklin shook his head. During his many years as secretary and as a member of the Assembly he had learned to be patient.

"Haste makes waste," he said, quoting Poor Richard.

The Indians wanted to make the boundaries — the frontiers — clear. They wanted the English colonists to stay on the east side of the mountains.

At last, after four days, the commissioners started back to Philadelphia. They rode over hills and through valleys and along streams. The leaves were turning to bright autumn colors. "It is a beautiful land," Franklin remarked. "It all belonged to the Indians once. No wonder they are concerned about keeping boundaries."

Franklin had been impressed with the way the group of Indian tribes called the Six Nations had worked together. "Our colonies should be able to do as well as savage Indian tribes," he pointed out. He believed the colonies should bind themselves together more closely.

When Franklin arrived home he found a new job waiting for him. He had been appointed by England as deputy postmaster general for all the colonies. Mail was delivered by horseback. Service was so slow and cost so much that few people used it. Franklin set to work to make the postal service good, fast, and reasonably priced. "A good postal service will do more than anything else to unite the colonies," he said.

Franklin was appointed to meet the Indians at Albany to renew pledges of peace. On his way he wrote down a plan of union for the colonies. But the plan was not adopted.

Before long the colonists had a real problem of defense against raids. The Indians were coming within a hundred miles of Philadelphia. Slipping past the frontier towns, they were scalping and killing whole families. Franklin rode west at the head of an expedition of soldiers. They built three forts to protect the colonists against the Indians.

Soon after that journey the Assembly of Pennsylvania appointed Franklin to go to England to try to get fairer taxes for the colony.

Franklin was not anxious to go. He was planning to build a new house. He wanted to watch its construction.

"Be sure all the chimneys are made properly," he cautioned Debbie. "And be sure lightning rods are attached immediately."

The morning he was sailing for England, Franklin heard shouts outside his window. Looking out, he saw hundreds of soldiers lined up. They were the men who had gone to the west with him to build the new forts.

"We want Franklin!" they cried. When Franklin appeared at the door they cheered.

"You know, men, I am no good at speech-making," Franklin said. "But I am very pleased that you came to tell me good-by."

Franklin was taking William with him. He promised Debbie and Sally he would send them some fine presents from England.

The voyage to England took almost four months. During it, Franklin had time to write part of his new almanac. He used many of his earlier sayings. He also wrote the books later known as *Father Abraham's Speech* and *The Way to Wealth*. *The Way to Wealth* contained good advice which thrifty Americans loved. "Lost time is never found again," Franklin wrote. "Always taking out of the meal-tub and never putting in soon comes to the bottom."

As soon as the Franklins arrived in London, they took a sightseeing trip. Then William was enrolled in Oxford University to study law.

Franklin did not forget his promise to Debbie and Sally. He laughed as he bought china and silver which he knew Debbie would love. He was remembering the first china bowl and silver spoon Debbie had bought for him many years before!

Franklin spent several years in London, working for the good of the colonies in America. In spite of his efforts and great wisdom, the American colonists and England disagreed more and more bitterly. The Stamp Act placed a tax on almost everything the colonists used. This act made the colonists angrier than ever. They believed that taxation without the power to help make the laws — representation — was unfair.

Franklin arrived home in Philadelphia in May, 1775. It was a sad homecoming, for Debbie had died several months before. Fighting had already broken out at Lexington and Concord. Franklin realized that his efforts to keep peace were useless. He knew that his beloved colonies and their mother country, England, were on the brink of war.

CHAPTER THIRTEEN

• LIFE, LIBERTY, HAPPINESS •

Franklin was a member of the new Continental Congress, the Assembly of the thirteen American colonies. He had come to believe, with other American patriots, that the colonies must gain their freedom from England. To do this, he knew that they must get supplies and help from some country other than England. How and where could they get the help they needed?

The world was watching the American colonies. France, especially, was interested. She wanted their trade. But France was England's powerful rival, and England did not want her colonies to have any trade with

France. So England tried to keep American ports closed, except to her own ships.

During 1775 and 1776, Franklin worked even harder than usual. He wrote to a friend: "In the morning at six I am at the Committee of Safety till near nine, when I am at the Congress, and that sits till after four in the afternoon." Soon Franklin's work for the colonies lasted far into the nights, too.

Since Debbie's death, Sally and her husband, Richard Bache, and their children had come to live with Franklin. They helped fill the new house on Market Street and make it home for him. There were many visitors, too. They came from near and far to see the great man they called Doctor Franklin.

One evening a French bookseller came to call on Franklin. As soon as they were alone the Frenchman looked about cautiously. "Can we be overheard?" he asked. "I have come on a mission of utmost delicacy."

"My daughter who met you at the door, her husband, my two grandchildren, and a servant are the only persons here," said Franklin, "but you may close the door. Please excuse me for not getting up. My gout troubles me so much these days."

The Frenchman closed the door to Franklin's study. A moment later he told Franklin that a French agent, appointed by the King of France, wished to talk with him. The meetings must be in strictest secrecy.

Franklin drew a deep breath. "It is a great honor," he said, "but it is a great responsibility." He studied the man carefully. The bookseller might be a British spy. But the colonists needed aid badly. At last Franklin said, "Of course I will meet your agent. But you know, we could both be hanged for this!"

During the next weeks Franklin had many secret meetings with the French agent. He arranged for the agent to meet other members of the Safety Committee. These men were torn between hope and doubt. They were never absolutely sure that they were dealing with a real agent of the French government. The agent had not dared to bring any written identification.

If the colonists wanted help from France, he said, they must declare their independence from England. The American colonists were afraid to declare independence until they were sure of help from France. They had nothing except their trade to offer France in return for help. And for helping the colonists, France risked a war with England.

Franklin wrote many letters to Europe, trying to get information. But his letters had to be so cautious that he learned little.

At last the Congress decided that help from France was America's only hope of freedom from England's unfair treatment. In December, 1775, the committee promised that Congress would declare independence.

On New Year's Day, 1776, the British burned Norfolk, Virginia. After this, feeling in the colonies grew hotter. Early in June, a committee was appointed by Congress to write a declaration of independence from England.

Franklin, John Adams, and Thomas Jefferson were on the committee. Jefferson did most of the writing. When he had finished, he took the declaration to Franklin to read.

Carefully Franklin read the declaration. He paused at several places. Then he looked up at Jefferson, who sat waiting uneasily.

Franklin's smile was warm. "I like it. It is simple. It is dignified. And it has beauty. I would suggest only a few little changes."

Before the declaration was signed by Congress many suggestions were made. It was clear that everyone there would have written it differently. At last Franklin spoke up.

As he told a humorous story the members of the Congress began to relax. Smiles took the place of frowns, for everyone loved Franklin's gentle good humor. At last the members realized that a single declaration could not satisfy everyone completely. They voted to accept the declaration as it was.

President of the Congress, John Hancock, was the first to sign. He wrote with a bold stroke of his pen. "There must be no pulling in different ways," he said. "We must all hang together."

Then Franklin's cheery voice added, "Yes, we must all hang together or most assuredly we shall all hang separately."

It was July 4, 1776, when the Continental Congress approved the Declaration of Independence. A new government, the United States of America, was born. Only Franklin and a few other patriots knew the months of strain and secret diplomacy that had helped the new nation to life.

On July 8, at noon, all the bells of Philadelphia rang out. People, young and old, gathered before the red brick building called the State House. They heard the secretary read the Declaration of Independence.

The words rang out clear and true and simple. At last the position of the Americans was defined. They would not stand England's abuses. If necessary, they would fight for their liberty. Cheers rose in great waves and filled the air. When Franklin returned home to sit in his garden he could still hear them.

A young voice broke in on his thoughts. "Grandpa, what does the Declaration of Independence mean?" Young Benjamin Franklin Bache, seven years old, pulled at his grandfather's sleeve.

Franklin hesitated for a moment. How could he make his grandson understand? Then he smiled. "Why, it means just what it says — the right to life, liberty, and the pursuit of happiness!"

CHAPTER FOURTEEN

• AMBASSADOR TO FRANCE •

Benjamin Franklin was seventy years old when the Declaration of Independence was signed. His health was poor. Often he had trouble in getting around. Still, no one thought of him as an old man.

The United States of America, the new nation, was already at war with Great Britain. General George Washington and his ragged soldiers needed food, clothing, and ammunition to carry on the war. Who could be sent to France to try to get help and get it fast?

The men in Congress looked around. "Benjamin Franklin," they said. "He is known all over the world as a great scientist. His *Poor*

Richard's Almanac is known also. He is a patriot who has won the admiration of the French already. Benjamin Franklin is the one to send to France!"

Franklin had learned as a young man that help offered and help given were two different things. He knew that it would be a hard job to get France to give enough help to America. But when Congress asked him to go to France he could not refuse.

He asked William's son, Temple, to go with him. Temple was seventeen years old and Franklin hoped to train him to be his secretary.

"Let me go, too," pleaded Franklin's namesake, Benny Bache. "I won't be any trouble."

Benny was only seven, and he and his grandfather were great pals. Franklin had dreaded leaving him. Benny begged and begged. At last Franklin said, "Ask your mother. If she says yes, you may come along."

To Franklin's surprise Sally agreed to let Benny go. Tears filled her eyes, but she said, "I know he will be a comfort to you, Pa, and he will learn a great deal."

Franklin collected all the money he could raise and gave it to Congress to use. Then, with his two grandsons, Temple and Benny, he sailed for France on an armed ship, the *Reprisal*. The ship's crew feared English ships might learn that Franklin was on board and try to capture the *Reprisal*. So they zigzagged across the Atlantic. Cold winds and storms tossed the ship about. But the British did not find it. At last, on December 3, the ship docked on the French shore.

Franklin hired a carriage to take them inland. It was cold and rickety and the roads were rough. It was a terrible trip. As they drove through a dense forest the driver spoke excitedly in French.

"What did he say, Grandpa?" Benny asked.

"A band of robbers lives in these woods. Two weeks ago they attacked some travelers right here. Are you afraid?"

"No, Grandpa," Benny answered bravely.

Franklin smiled. He put his arm around the boy. Soon Benny was asleep on his grandfather's shoulder. And the carriage rolled along unharmed.

In Paris a great welcome awaited Franklin. The French people took him to their hearts. Nobles and peasants — men, women, and children — turned out in the streets to cheer him.

"*Vive le Franklin! Vive le Franklin!*" they cried.

"*Vive la France!*" Franklin answered.

"This warmhearted, liberty-loving American speaks our language," they cried delightedly.

Franklin was even more popular in France than he had been at home. Pictures of him were everywhere. A fine statue of him was made and bore these words: "He snatched the lightning from the sky and the sceptre from tyrants."

"You give me too much credit," Franklin said. "It is only with the help of many brave men in the Revolution that we can hope to win independence from the king's rule."

Franklin's house in Passy, just outside Paris, was a busy place, always filled with the many friends he had interested in helping the Americans win their liberty. Many French people gave their own money. One young nobleman, the Marquis de Lafayette, not only gave his money. He crossed the ocean to join General Washington, and served as an officer in the Revolutionary Army.

One day Benny ran into his grandfather's study. "Grandpa! Grandpa! John Paul Jones is here," he cried excitedly.

"He is just the young man I want to meet," said Franklin. This was the beginning of a good friendship. Franklin admired the daring young seaman who believed the Americans must raid the British coasts and defeat the king's men at sea.

Jones and Franklin agreed that the British ships which carried supplies to the British soldiers in America must be stopped. Jones wanted Franklin's help in securing armed ships from France.

At last, in 1779, Jones sailed out to sea to stop the British ships in their own waters. Jones named his ship the *Bonhomme Richard* in honor of his good friend, Franklin. It became one of the noblest ships in history. Manned by Jones and his men, it helped to give Americans new hope for victory.

Franklin worked hard to secure all kinds of help from France. At last a treaty was signed with the French government. Then

the French king, Louis XVI, invited Franklin
and other Americans who were in Paris seek-
ing help for America to come to his palace.

Franklin wore an old brown velvet suit and
white stockings. His thin hair hung loose to
his shoulders. His spectacles rested on his

nose. They were bifocals which he had invented so that he could see objects both near and far. Franklin seemed plainly dressed in comparison to the other guests at the palace.

But the people lined up outside the palace were waiting not to see them, but Franklin. They cheered as he passed.

The French king smiled as he shook Franklin's hand. "Assure Congress of my friendship," he said.

All the ladies wanted to meet Franklin, and the queen stood proudly beside him. He smiled at the great nobles and the ladies in court.

Franklin was proud to have the United States of America recognized as a nation. And he was relieved that France had pledged more help. His kind face glowed with happiness. Now he felt confident the American colonists would win their fight for liberty.

CHAPTER FIFTEEN

• THE RISING SUN •

At last, after years of fighting and sacrifice, war with England was over. With France's help the colonists had won, and the United States was a free nation. After almost ten years in France, Benjamin Franklin was coming home. He left the French people in tears. He had been with them so long they felt that he belonged to them.

In Philadelphia cannons boomed. Bells rang. Flags waved. "Welcome home, Benjamin Franklin," the people waiting shouted. All Philadelphia had turned out to meet her favorite citizen — the most famous man in the whole world.

How good it was to come home! Franklin kissed his daughter and the new grandchildren, born while he was in France. The crowd cheered Franklin all the way to his home. It cheered him as patriot, statesman, inventor, and as the everyday character it seemed to love most of all — Poor Richard.

Franklin's grandsons, both grown tall, shared in the honors of his welcome.

"Temple has become a French gentleman. He knows only the diplomatic life," Franklin said a little sadly. Then he looked with satisfaction at Benny. He was glad that he had hired a man to teach Benny printing in France. "I wish I had taught Temple a trade, too," he said.

Franklin's return was celebrated for more than a week. "The affectionate welcome from my fellow citizens," Franklin wrote a friend, "was far beyond my expectations."

Franklin's work in France was over. But

work on the problems of the free nation was just beginning. Franklin believed that, to keep its freedom, the United States must make a plan of government. It must be a strong plan to hold the states together. It must be a democratic plan to preserve the ideas of the Declaration of Independence.

In May, 1787, a convention of fifty-five men met to write a plan of government for the United States of America. This plan was to be called the Constitution. The men in this Constitutional Convention represented the different colonies, now called states. They spent months on the Constitution — months of thinking, working, planning, arguing. They wanted the Constitution to be the best plan of government they could make.

The meetings were held in the red brick State House in Philadelphia. Many of the same men who had signed the Declaration of Independence eleven years before were there. Franklin, of course, was there. Usually he sat quietly, listening to the arguments.

After they had been meeting for four months, Franklin believed that the Convention should finish its work. On September 17, the Constitution was read once more to the Convention.

Benjamin Franklin, now 81 years old, reached for his cane and rose painfully to his feet. The room was hushed. The men waited. They knew that the Convention would be guided by the wisdom of Franklin's words.

Franklin handed a written speech to James Wilson of Pennsylvania to read. The words seemed to ring through the quiet room:

"There are several parts of this Constitution which I do not at present approve. But I am not sure I shall never approve them."

Franklin meant that, as time passed, he might be convinced of the wisdom of all parts. How wise! How true! The delegates nodded.

"The older I grow," Franklin's words went on, "the more apt I am to doubt my own judgment and to pay attention to the judgment of others."

Then he pointed out that most people in an argument were like the French lady who said to her sister, " 'I don't know why it is, sister, but I meet with nobody but myself that's always in the right.' "

The men chuckled over the story. Once more Franklin had made them laugh. More important, he had made them understand an idea. He had shown them that every man could not expect to agree with every part of the Constitution.

Then, suddenly, came Franklin's stirring words: "I agree to this Constitution with all its faults, if they are such; because I think a general government necessary for us. And there is no form of government but what may be a blessing to the people if well administered." Then, simply, he asked all the delegates to sign.

On that day, September 17, 1787, most of the delegates signed the Constitution. Franklin signed his name with a flourish that had become famous, but it was still firm and true as ever. He smiled at his good friend, George Washington, presiding at the meeting. Thoughtfully, his eyes kept going back to the chair in which Washington was sitting. The high back was carved in deep lines which looked like the rays of the sun.

Franklin turned to James Madison, sitting beside him. "Many times during this Convention I have wondered whether the sun on that chair represented the United States as a rising sun or a setting sun," he said. "But now I know at last. It is a *rising* sun!"

Soon the delegates began to leave the State House. Franklin was a little tired. It would feel good to be at home just sitting in his garden under the big old mulberry tree and listening to the happy voices of his grand-children and the neighbors' children. They would grow up in a free country that he had helped to make.

Benjamin Franklin smiled. It was a smile of kindness, of wisdom, of contentment.